Finding our voice

Our truth, community and journey
as Australian Young Friends

2010
THE **JAMES BACKHOUSE** LECTURE

Finding our voice

Our truth, community and journey
as Australian Young Friends

Quakers
AUSTRALIA

Produced by Australia Yearly Meeting of the Religious Society of Friends (Quakers) in Australia Incorporated

Typesetting by Neville Ross

Printed by Uniprint, Hobart

National Library of Australia Cataloguing-in-Publication entry:

Title: Finding our voice : our truth, community and journey as
            Australian young friends / Australian
            Young Friends (Quakers).

ISBN: 9780980325867 (pbk.)

Series: James Backhouse Lecture.

Subjects: Spiritual life--Quakers.
            Quakers--Attitudes.
            Quakers--Australia.
            Youth--Australia.

Other Authors/Contributors:
            Australian Young Friends (Quakers).

Dewey Number: 289.6994

Copies may be ordered from:
Friends Book Sales, PO Box 181
Glen Osmond SA 5064 Australia.
Email: sales@quakers.org.au

About the authors

We all had different involvement at different times, but it was all important and it's what made this lecture what it is today. In naming those who have been involved, there is a risk that we will miss someone's name. If we have, our humble apologies and heartfelt thanks for your contribution to this process.

Lewis Albanis
Kate Barnard
Paul Barnier
Callista Barritt
Jerome Barty-Taylor
Miranda Barty-Taylor
Gareth Beyers
Connor Chaffey
Emily Chapman-Searle
Hannah Chapman-Searle
Rhys Dryzek
Aletia Dundas
Tom Dundas
Esther Fox
Sam Fry
Evan Gallagher
Amber Goedegebuure
Oliver Greeves

Bethany Growns
Verity Guiton
Imogen Hamel-Green
Chris Hall
Herman Itangakubuntu
Chris Jacques
Nadia Johnson
Stuart Johnson
Sally Kingsland
Cammie Kelly
Peter Kneale
Antoinette Kwizera
Dale Lund
Jess Lund (nee Dundas)
Julie Martin
Kerensa McElroy
Melchiade Nishimwe
Adolf (Niyo) Niyonkuru

Caroline Plunkett
Kyle Purnell
Jensen Sass
Megan Sheard
Katana Smith
Sally Stokes
Warren Summers
Alexa Taylor
Jo Temme
Amy Thom
Aline Vyizigiro
Emily Walpole
Mary Webb
Rachael Westwood
Myf White
Ailsa Wild
Anna Wilkinson
Ben Williamson

Acknowledgments

There are many, many people who have been part of this process in all kinds of ways. We are eternally grateful to you all.

To the Backhouse Lecture Committee, concurrently a stroke of madness and genius to invite us to embark on this journey.

To the people we live with who were invaded by Backhousers time and time again, thank you for the space, the food, the cups of tea, the love and support. We are so grateful.

To Canberra Meeting and our Canberra-based support committee, thank you for being willing every time we asked for assistance and for holding us in our endeavours.

To the Canberra Young Friends, from the rest of us, thank you for guiding us on this wonderful journey, and making it a rewarding and joyous one to be part of.

To all our friends and family, thank you for loving us, supporting us and putting up with us!

Finally, we are thankful for that which connects us and binds us together in this deliciously messy adventure we are on.

ontents

Dear reader

This lecture is the result of a year and a half collaboration between many people in many places. We have worked to find 'our voice' and along the way have had more adventures, struggles, delights, 'ah-ha' moments, fun, tears, challenges, support and love than can be captured in words. This lecture holds many voices; they are individual voices, united voices and created voices. Collectively they are our voice. Please don't spend too much time trying to work out which voice is which; it's not important and sometimes is not actually possible. Throughout the lecture there are a number of dialogues. These are between characters we have created; they do not represent specific individuals.

'Young Friends' is the name given to people aged 16 to 30-ish who have a connection with the Religious Society of Friends (Quakers). Yet the term has come to represent a particular group of people—those involved right now in the Australian Young Friends group. And so this is our story. This lecture is a snapshot of our group at a particular point in time.

When Young Friends collectively accepted the invitation to give the lecture, the first question we had to answer was, 'How?'. We didn't want this Backhouse Lecture to be a collection of individual writings, but rather a structured message delivered with a single consistent voice. How are Young Friends to collectively speak as one? How do we go about agreeing on what the lecture should be about? How do we involve all Young Friends around Australia?

We have been blessed by technology, and have relied heavily on email and Skype to help us stay in touch with each other. However, nothing can replace the importance of face-to-face time, and we have made time and space for many gatherings around the country during this process.

Soliciting contributions meant being prepared to accept them and handle them with appropriate care. The Canberra Young Friends group (who agreed to hold the process of creating the lecture, and later the writing of it) asked Young Friends around Australia to share their experiences of being a Young Friend, and have been privileged to be entrusted with people's stories. In discussions around the Backhouse process we regularly wondered how to best reflect the contributions in a coherent whole, finding the balance between summarising and de-identifying versus allowing Young Friends' words to stand for themselves. In the end, our goal is to present a piece of work in which every contributor can see evidence of their contributions, and which every Young Friend agrees reflects the truth and the diversity of what the Young Friends community is all about.

Working on the Backhouse Lecture has been difficult but rewarding. It's a challenging task that has given us something to focus on, drawing in people who might otherwise have had less involvement in Young Friends. Sometimes we muse on what the Young Friends community in Australia will look like post-Backhouse, or what we might have looked like without it.

Working towards the Backhouse Lecture has involved substantial contributions of time. Most Young Friends are busy people, and while facilitating or contributing to a Quaker lecture is not always the highest priority, we have all created 'Backhouse' space in our life over the last year and a half. Creating the space for Backhouse discussions and attracting people into that space have been key parts of the process. We distributed prompting questions, shared contributions with each other, held writing workshops, facilitated sessions with games and community-building techniques, interviewed each other, gathered at camps, and asked people to express themselves by drawing, all to create opportunities to share stories and perspectives with each other and to capture contributions that could serve as the foundation for the lecture.

Much like a Regional Meeting minute, this lecture is the product of discernment. When the final draft of this lecture is approved for printing, there will not be a room containing every Young Friend from around Australia, all of whom have read it carefully in order to endorse it. Successive drafts have been distributed via email, and many Young Friends offered feedback resulting in changes in new drafts. And at some point a draft will become the final one.

One theme that has emerged strongly is: 'Whose Friends are we?'. Are we just a social group of friends? What role does the Religious Society of Friends play in our lives? Do we feel we are friends with older Quakers? Or are we, like the early Quakers, simply young 'Friends of the Truth', striving to live our lives with integrity?

We invite you to share with us an attempt to answer some of these questions through an exploration of what it means to call oneself a Young Friend; how we relate to one another; how we relate to Quakers; and how we relate to the outside world. Within this framework we explore the expectations placed on us as young people within a spiritual community, what we want from this community, the importance of play, the challenges we face in living out our beliefs, and our hopes for the future. Join us — it will be fun.

Who are Young Friends?

A Young Friend is a young Friend is a Young friend is a young friend.

> *Young Friends are like 'fellow explorers' — we support each other on our journey.*

Gertrude Stein wrote 'A rose is a rose is a rose is a rose' in her poem 'Sacred Emily'. The repetition in this sentence has been said to invoke the true meaning of a rose, and Stein herself said that in this sentence the rose is red for the first time in English poetry. It also encourages us to ponder the question, 'What IS A ROSE to us?'

We don't presume to have all the answers to what a rose is, or even what a Young Friend is; however, the process of writing the 2010 Backhouse Lecture has taken us all on a journey of discovery of what Young Friends means to us. We recognise that Young Friends is certainly not just one Young Friend, or even one belief, or even one thought. To come closer to understanding what a Young Friend is, we must hear what Young Friends means to each and every one of us. While we don't all necessarily agree on anything, by bringing all the Young Friends' voices together, the true meaning of Young Friend is clearer and we can hear one voice.

The current group of Australian Young Friends can be traced back more than a decade, to around the time of Perth Yearly Meeting 1998. Some of us have been attending Young Friends gatherings and events for this entire time, some have joined since then and some have moved on from Young Friends.

We have had a few pivotal moments along the way. In Perth, Young Friends and Junior Young Friends came together to write the 'Young People's Statement' about our experience of being young people in Australia Yearly Meeting. At Yearly Meeting in Brisbane in 2000 we ran a Summer School called 'From isolation to inclusion'. At Yearly Meeting in Tasmania in 2007 Young Friends were challenged as a group about the way we operate, our own processes of exclusion and inclusion, as well as the diversity of the Young Friend experience.

One of the things that has come to characterise this group is our desire to be involved in the life of the Yearly Meeting. An example of this is the fact that there are two places on most Yearly Meeting committees designated for Young Friends.

Various local groups in various locations have brought together Young Friends for gatherings of a spiritual and social nature to try to add more local opportunities for community building. The most recent example of this is the Canberra group, whose story you can read in Appendix 1.

The Young Friends community is, in some ways, just a microcosm of the broader Society. A lot of the concerns we talk about, and a lot of the things that inspire us, will sound familiar to Quakers. We are diverse, like Quakers as a whole. We have varying levels of knowledge about Quakerism, and varying levels of interest in the spiritual, social justice or just plain social aspects of Quakers. We are explorers, each on our own spiritual journey, and we find that having some company on the way can teach us new things and help us through the rough patches.

Spiritual community

Although we have many things in common with the broader Quaker family, it is important to note that Young Friends is a distinct and unique expression of spiritual community. We are not just a mini-Quaker gathering and neither are we simply a social club. We are also not a spiritual community in the traditional sense; that is, a group of people bound together by a common belief. Rather, we are a community of young people exploring spirituality and life together, within an identifiably Quaker context.

We create a place for young people to experiment with, and draw from the Society's unwritten rules and written history, as we explore our spirituality as individuals and as a community. As one Young Friend said:

> *I feel like I get things from Young Friends that aren't available in the wider Quaker community. That's why I stick around — for the ability to have spiritual conversations that aren't really structured. I don't have conversations that challenging anywhere else.*

We recognise that Quakers have varied beliefs. For many of us this is what attracted us to Quakers, and is what sets Quakers apart from many other religious traditions. However, as a Young Friends community we experience a great tension between creating a diverse culture, embracing a broad range of beliefs within Young Friends, and maintaining our Quaker identity.

This freedom of belief and acceptance of everyone means that there is naturally a reluctance to articulate exactly what we believe, both individually and collectively. Without a corporate spiritual identity, we struggle with questions about who we are. While not having a creed serves to encourage a broader range of seekers to Quakers, it also raises the question 'What do you need to believe to be a Quaker?'. One Young Friend thought the catchphrase for Quakerism could be 'No God, No Problem'.

Choosing to be involved with Quakers entails either being comfortable with some ambiguity or determining one's own views, belief and identity.

However, even with these struggles for identity, Young Friends still find immense value in being together as a spiritual community, whether exclusively as Young Friends, or as members of the broader Quaker community.

> *Quakerism gives me the language I need to consider my spiritual journey, the framework to begin exploring questions about conflict in the world.*

Finally, as a unique spiritual community actively involved in the broader Quaker context, we hope that our journeys and stories will move the whole Society in new and exciting ways.

> *I feel that Quakerism will change as the group of people our age grow into being 'older' (weightier?!) Quakers over the decades to come. Sometimes in local Meetings I feel that there is almost a pre-ordained set of rules and beliefs that must be taken on. I feel with Young Friends (perhaps like all younger generations), we feel more free to question these traditional beliefs and maybe even those 'issues that Quakers must have a certain view on'. In doing so, we come up with our own views, which I don't think are any less spiritual or any less valid. In fact, sometimes letting go of the way we are used to doing things and being free to explore new ways is being more open for the spirit to move more freely and guide Quakerism to where it's going. That's pretty exciting.*

Young Friends and Quaker identities

As Young Friends, we share the values and ideals of the Quaker community including the testimonies of simplicity, peace, integrity, community and equality. How these values and ideals are acted upon and emphasised varies from Young Friend to Young Friend.

I don't like the idea of having to do something because I'm a Quaker and 'that's what Quakers do'. To me it's more a case that I do this and that, and because I do them, that makes me a Quaker. It's the same with beliefs. I feel that because I believe what I believe, I'm a Quaker, not that, because I'm a Quaker therefore I believe.

Some of us call ourselves Quakers because we are convinced Friends, sometimes expressed also through being members of the Religious Society of Friends. Others of us call ourselves Quakers because we were brought up by Quakers and it is our family and cultural heritage. Sometimes we identify as Quakers because of the association we feel with other people who call themselves Quakers whom we respect and whose beliefs are consistent with our own.

By calling myself a Quaker I feel like I am part of a community within which a spiritually rich life is considered an achievable and worthwhile goal, something to search for and work towards. I am proud of Quakers searching for this through history.

Others of us do not consider ourselves Quakers at all, but strongly identify as, or appreciate being associated with, Young Friends. Although some of us choose not to label ourselves as a Quaker, we still embrace Quaker values in our own lives. The reasons for not calling ourselves 'Quakers' include our choice not to be active in a local Meeting or the broader Society, or a general disinclination to be associated with a religious group. There are also Young Friends who have a Quaker heritage from countries other than Australia, such as Burundi, who feel more comfortable identifying as 'Friends' rather than 'Quakers'.

Sometimes Young Friends hold the weighty Quakers in such high regard that it feels presumptuous to identify ourselves as a Quaker alongside these amazing people. Conversely, we appreciate Young Friends as a place where we can be part of a community that is informed by Quaker values, and where we can explore spiritual growth without the formalities that are often associated with the Society, and without the pressure to feel like a 'true Quaker'.

Beyond how we self-identify as Quakers, Friends, Young Friends or not at all, how we express that to others who are not familiar with the Society reveals a lot. In today's secular society where the media tends to portray religion dominated by fundamentalism, there is a strong reluctance to identify with a religious body. As one Young Friend says:

> *I never tell people I'm a Quaker. Not unless I know them really well. Whenever an opportunity comes up to tell someone about my Quakerism, a wave of fear comes over me: 'What if they think I'm crazy and don't like me anymore?'!*

And yet, once we get past the reluctance to associate with a religious institution, we often find that talking about it can be very valuable. The same Young Friend goes on to say:

> *When I look back on the times that I have talked about my Quakerism to non-Quakers, I realise that the good experiences vastly outweigh the bad ones; it's just that negative experiences tend to stay on my mind.*

Because of the amount of time spent together, and the strong friendships built, there is a real depth to relationships within Young Friends, an extra level of trust and openness. Some Young Friends feel that if Young Friends had membership, they would be there in a heartbeat, yet have not chosen to join the Religious Society of Friends (yet!).

We feel that Young Friends should be seen as worthwhile on its own, and not expected to 'recruit' young people for the Religious Society of Friends. Young Friends gatherings provide a space in which people can just 'be' and explore their spirituality with other young people who are open to exploration. This would not be possible, though, without the broader framework and traditions of the Society of Friends.

Whose Friend are Young Friends?

Arthur: So we've been talking about Young Friends all this time. This might seem pretty basic, but why do we call ourselves this? Are Young Friends just Quakers who are young?

Beryl: *For me, a Young Friend really is just a Quaker who is young. I started attending Meeting before I heard of Young Friends. I was one of the only Young Friends in my local Meeting. It was great to start attending Young Friends gatherings later, but for me 'Young Friends' is just a purely descriptive label.*

Arthur: Yeah, that makes sense.

Clive: It does, but not all Young Friends identify as 'Quakers'. I've attended Young Friends camp, and Junior Young Friends before that, for years. These have been some of the most important years of my life. The friendships have been some of the deepest I've experienced, even though we only see each other a couple of times a year, and have shaped the way I look at things.

Arthur: So you don't see yourself as a Quaker?

Clive: Not really. I haven't got into the whole 'Quaker' thing of going to Meeting for Worship and being on committees. I haven't felt this need in my life. But Young Friends are still very important to me.

Arthur: Right. So we can't assume Young Friends are all just young Quakers. But we still use the word 'Friend' ...

Beryl: *I don't see a problem with that. 'Friend' used to be shorthand for 'Friend of Truth'. For me, it still is. I like to think anyone can be a Friend of Truth, not just Quakers.*

Arthur: Nice. I'm not sure we all use the word this way, though. I think I'm like a lot of Quakers, and use the word because it is the traditional label. I'm not really sure if there is more to it for me right now.

Doris: *I'm not even sure what a Quaker is. I grew up overseas and attended a Friends' Church. We didn't use the word 'Quaker'. We learnt all about how to live based on the Gospels, but now I'm in Australia I don't know how to live as a Quaker. I'm not sure what it means to be a Quaker.*

Being together

The true experience of Young Friends lies in how we 'do' community. Our Young Friends community aims to provide a safe and supportive platform from which we can launch ourselves. This safe, supportive and inspiring space is one of the most important aspects of Young Friends, as it provides a place where we can explore parts of ourselves that we may not feel able to in other places.

Young Friends was also a space where I felt entirely accepted,
had my beliefs and values challenged and shaped.

This community gives us the confidence and inspiration to go out and live in the world. It is also a place to come back to, to refresh our ideas, renew our enthusiasm for life and find that spark that motivates us to let our lives speak every day.

However, we recognise that we all fall short of this ideal from time to time. We are aware that there are people who aren't with Young Friends now because they do feel they have been judged or excluded. It is difficult to balance having a close community with deep relationships that have been built up over years with being open to newcomers who change and enrich our group.

Camp

Camp is an essential time for the Australian Young Friends community. Camps are usually held twice a year, one immediately before Yearly Meeting and one at Easter time. These camps range from four to seven days, are loosely structured, and have a focus on us being together in community. The community building that naturally happens when we live together for several days is one of the reasons that camps are such an important time for Young Friends.

Over those ten days my voice became bigger as night after night we sang round after round, song after song. Sitting in the bathrooms for hours bouncing harmony off concrete. Splashing in sunset waves with our voices raised until dark. I taught people how to play chords on the guitar. One evening we stood in a circle at the nearby marina, dressed in daggy clothes that we had been wearing all week and not caring one bit, and sang our songs for the world outside.

Time

At Young Friends camps we create community by giving ourselves the gift of time: time to be, time to grow, time to play. At camps we have a lot of unprogrammed, unstructured and spontaneous time. This time is filled with...

fun, games, conversations, adventures, silliness, seriousness, laughing, crying, cooking, eating, swimming, singing...

These things that we do in our unprogrammed time are a very important part of our community building and allow us to form deep connections with each other. They also help us in being more present with each other in our programmed time.

Often the gaps in between the things in the agenda are the times that are most fulfilling.

Our loose structure also means that we do things at Young Friends camps that we don't do in our everyday life. We can stay up all night playing games and then decide to drive to the top of the mountain nearby to watch the sunrise! These are things we wouldn't do in our everyday life because we don't give ourselves the time to, and yet when we do them at camps, these experiences are unforgettable.

The amount of time that we spend together is also a key aspect in our community building. When we gather for our camps we spend several days or even a week together. Living together, cooking together, eating together, often sleeping in shared spaces. Living together in this way means that we get to know each other on a very deep level—much more than if we were just spending a week together in a non-residential program. We learn who likes to stay up late, who likes to get up early, who loves to cook, who will always be able to have their arm twisted into just one more game of 500!

At camps, our time together is devoted solely to being with Young Friends. We often gather in the bush or in a small town—away from the distractions of cities. We spend all our time in the same place with the same people, and over the week the place becomes home and the people become family.

While Young Friends camps are loosely structured, we are also very careful about ensuring that there are times when the whole group gathers together. Playing games as a whole group is one example of this. We also eat dinner together as a group every night, preferably with all of us sitting around the one table. Epilogues are also a precious group time, and while we don't always have epilogues every night, when we do have them they are often a deep and spiritual time of sharing and bonding. Without these intentional group times together, the group can become fragmented, and people could easily end up feeling isolated and left out.

Space

Another important aspect in creating and sustaining our community is the space we create.

There is some unknown force that brings everyone together at a Young Friends camp, no matter age, race or gender. I have seen it happen time and time again. The space that is created is so safe, beautiful and inspiring that it is sometimes hard to imagine anything better.

A safe space allows us to be real and open with each other.

Young Friends is a space in which we can be vulnerable. Through play, living in close space, being silly, being creative through music and art and trying new things, being challenged by each other. Talking about things that matter makes us vulnerable.

Many feel that this is a space in which it is easier to be themselves.

Young Friends camps provide a space in which I feel safe to share my gifts and be myself. This doesn't happen by chance. We have to pay attention to the group and to each individual so that the space is held in this way. It's not always easy, but it's always worth it.

This space also offers a time to explore and examine who we are, and who we want to be.

I feel like Young Friends camps are a place where I can not only be myself, but also examine myself, a place where I can make changes in my life if there are things that I want to change.

There is a spontaneous openness and trust when we meet in Young Friends settings.

The space has to be safe, and it usually is. But it also has to be challenging and it always has been for me.

Camp can be a really important time away from the world, a chance to really be present with each other.

Camp is a kind of retreat. We leave our day-to-day world to focus on internal nourishment in places of natural beauty. It's a space to mostly just 'be' and to be in community; I've seen this lead to new insights and deeper connections between people.

The time and space we give ourselves mean that, for many, close friendships are easier to form, and a sense of community is easier to find.

Difficulties with camp

Many Young Friends have talked about how when they first started attending camps, they were unsure of how they would fit in. For some, spending time with other Young Friends and being involved in group activities is enough to feel a part of the group. However, for others, fitting into the group is not so easy.

I think it's intrinsic to the close bond that some Young Friends have that when people come in they feel excluded. That bond has developed over the course of time that people have known each other. I've experienced it and I suppose I'm still experiencing it. If you've got a couple of people who are joined closely it takes time to disentangle [them] and splice a new person in... So there may now be times when I have feelings of not fitting in or uncertainty of where I fit in relation to other people but there is the knowledge that with time it will change.

And for another Young Friend:

> *I remember when I first came to camp and I didn't feel included and I didn't feel like it was a deliberate thing or anything but I did feel separate from the group. It was just from hanging out and being involved and developing friendships with people outside camp — so people from my state know me and laugh at me where other people wouldn't. I think when people know you it helps other people to know you. I don't think it was even from one camp that I started to feel included. I think it took more than that before I came to trust people.*

These are challenges that we need to be deliberate in responding to. It truly is one of the mixed blessings of having such a close community that it is appealing to those who aren't in it, and that it takes intentional effort to include new people.

Sustaining our community throughout the year

While camps and gatherings are intrinsic to our community, so too are the bonds that exist between us, that allow us to call on each other at all kinds of times. There are so many ways we can be in touch with each other these days — phone, email, text messages, Skype, Facebook and so on. We use these tools to help us stay in contact throughout the year.

Being accessible seems to be easier when we are part of a geographic group than at camp where there are established routines and friendships to be renewed between people who live far away from each other. Building stronger groups that meet regularly in our home towns is a way we have made this transition possible for more Young Friends recently. The regular gatherings provide a more frequent, less intense space than a camp to get to know others in the community over a period of time. However, it is often difficult to do this, as building a strong local Young Friends community needs a sufficient number of people to be sustainable—including having at least some who are well connected to, and frequent attenders at a local Meeting for Worship.

Learning from our Young Friends community

The Young Friends community is also a space for learning, teaching, new experiences and growing up.

One Young Friend talks of Young Friends as elders:

> *I'm not very active in my local Meeting so my experience of eldering is fairly limited to that which occurs in the Young Friends community.*
>
> *There are some Young Friends whom I consider as my elders. I can open my heart to them and talk to them about my leadings and doubts. They don't give me advice, but they do what Quakers do best: they listen and ask the occasional probing question.*
>
> *They inspire me with their ministry when we're just hanging out or during worship sharing. And they inspire me by the way they lead their lives. When I observe how they interact with the world, I feel honoured to know them and their example is a pattern for me to apply to my own life.*
>
> *I learn a lot at Young Friends gatherings and I teach a lot too. I've learned a lot about Quaker history and practices, I've learned what a gathered business meeting feels like. I've shared my experiences and learnt and taught games and songs. I've learnt new dhal recipes and I've taught a Young Friend how to cut onions!*
>
> *I come away from a Young Friends camp with so much enthusiasm for the adventures I get to have in my life. I've*

been told 'I love you' in hundreds of ways and I'm affirmed
by my elders/friends/Friends.

Young Friends also speak of new experiences they have had through their involvement in Young Friends, and how Young Friends has been an important part of their growing up.

> *My first Young Friends camp was in Perth, my home town,*
> *when I had just turned 16, and it was so exciting to me,*
> *meeting people who were like me when I felt like such an*
> *oddity at school ... vegetarians, women who didn't shave*
> *their legs ... just like me, it was so exciting!*

Another Young Friend says:

> *I've done heaps of growing up with Quakers. Camps are*
> *quite an intense time. Someone said: 'I did all my growing*
> *up at camp.' That's true of me as well. I started to think*
> *about Left politics, sexuality, God ... It was the context in*
> *which I grew up ... Young Friends is a place where I get to*
> *explore spirituality.*

Getting in touch with our creativity

Creativity has always been a part of the culture of Young Friends, and can express itself in many ways in different people. It does not matter whether one person is a better musician, poet or songwriter than another, what matters is that people feel free to express themselves in ways they may never have thought of before.

> *When I am around Young Friends, everyday activities such*
> *as cooking and cleaning are transformed into opportunities*
> *to express my creativity. I've never thought of myself as an*

overly creative person, and so it is refreshing and comforting
to be able to express my creativity in such ways.

Creativity in Young Friends is not something that is forced upon people, and people don't always make a conscious effort to be creative. It is something that just happens. It is perhaps related to creating a suitable environment in which people feel they can be creative.

Creativity for me is about the space; if I feel safe amongst
the people and the surroundings, I am much more inclined
to express my creativity.

In saying this, however, we must remember that some Young Friends are more inclined to express their creativity in more tangible ways, such as through music, art, circus or dance.

I think when I am writing songs, I am endeavouring to
access truth at its very purest within me, stripped bare of
the fuss and glamour that seems to veil so much of what we
are presented with in society. As I peer critically at myself
and the world around me, and try to express these musings
poetically and simply, and above all with integrity, I feel
released from normal pressures, and uplifted, as though
through the creative process I can appreciate life at its
fullest and truest. I think that's why creating anything
is so important to young people. We are able to access and
acknowledge strength, beauty, frailty, simplicity—elements
of life which might otherwise be obscured from view.

Importance of play

Young Friends spend a lot of time playing. We play because we like to play and we play as an intentional part of our community building. We play games as a way to break the ice; we find that gathering together on the first night of camp to play games and introduce ourselves to the group really sets the tone for the whole camp. It relaxes newcomers into their first Young Friends camp and helps set up the safe space for the whole of our time together. One Young Friend suggested that play is essential to bring people closer to one another, to relax people and to form strong bonds with each other. Through play we open ourselves up to the group and form connections with the group.

> *I really appreciate the existence of games as a structured way to hang out with people. You can just do it. You don't have to have a deep conversation or be funny. It's quality time that I know how to do and it's reliable. It's a way to hang out with someone you don't know how to hang out with.*

One particular aspect of play that Young Friends value is the use of name games, particularly at the start of gatherings, or when there are people present not known to everybody.

> *The name games that we play at the start of camp and during camp itself are so important to me. They give me the chance to relax, settle into the space and (more often than not) have a good laugh as well.*

Another Young Friend writes:

> *I began thinking about this concept in the context of spirituality and God. I thought to myself: 'Why is play so important to me?' It's so important because it brings out the best in people, letting their light shine out to the world. This is why play is so important in forming bonds between people—it brings out the best in them. I then thought about the idea of there being 'that of God in everyone'. It suddenly hit me; if there is that of God in everyone, and play time brings out the best in people, then*

play time must bring out God in everyone. We are seeing God in our fun, our excitement and our joy. We are in the presence of, and surrounded by God as we have fun.

Open source poetry

An example of how we explore creativity is in creating things together. The following poem was written by a group of Young Friends as part of the Backhouse process.

Verse North: The best most funnest day
As I woke up, I could hear laughing and singing–
'Do your crazy laugh!', someone said.
A beach trip filled with lazy sun drenched surf
and an ice cream filled sandcastle.
We hid a plastic, very realistic, life size python in her bed …
Young Friends camp at Werona on Easter Sunday.
*So, having done what ones like them, would and did do,
a cheeky, sun drenched, laughing group of
young friends went home to share the joy.*

Verse East: Discovery of myself
There is so much I don't know, I want to grow.
So I decided to begin my search in the kitchen, where
many surprising things are hiding
I discovered myself in the mirror, in all my infinite
glory, with many stupendous things.
Listening to the changing sound of footsteps as I
move past walls of different heights…
I am part of everything and everything is part of me.
Chorus
A four-legged green stool waits for a bum to sit on it
Hugs. Smiles. Laughs. Dreams. Food. Belief. Soul.
And how does the flock know when it is time to change direction?

The violin ambled down the empty country road thinking to itself,
'What if everyone sounded like me, what if everyone thought like me?

Verse South: Sound and Silence
It was the sum of the shimmering, buzzing parts,
Music is always in my head, even when everything else is silent.
For me, water is both sound and silence, it allows me to
deepen, but is not so silent that it distracts me.
The sound of the pen on the paper, the rush of the traffic outside,
the ticking of the clock. Is it ever really silent?
Whole body Listening.

Verse West: Dare to Dream
Utopia — a word with a thousand hopes, a million dreams,
anything imagined — in such detail — such clarity...
is it the same as the real?
Courageous leaps in life move your mind forward
And then she climbed the 'structure' and mounted the swing.
With eyes on the river beyond, she jumped
The dream. The reality. The difference. (question mark)

Living out into the world

The way we live in this world informs and is informed by our interactions with other Young Friends. The individual ways we let our lives speak vary between us, but what is common is that we are all trying. We try to make intentional decisions about how we live and where we use our energy. This includes the choices we make about work and our relationships with others. This means some of us do one thing for a variety of reasons, and some of us do totally different things for exactly the same reason. Living a life of integrity can be tough, but as one Young Friend says:

> … as far as not always being easy, I find it healthy to remember that living good, regardless of how hard it is, is rewarding — and for me, it's really the only option.

'Good' is about the way we carry ourselves, the choices we make and our motivations. The ways that we aim to make a positive contribution to the world are diverse and reflect the times we live in. Being part of Young Friends helps us to do this, as one Young Friend explains:

Young Friends is a space to practise being how I want to be in the world and where it's okay to bugger it up, because I know that people will keep loving me and that I can just try again.

Living with integrity

We aim to integrate our lives with our values and beliefs; to live with integrity. Influences on our life decisions include the Quaker testimonies, a commitment to nature and other people, and the need to nurture ourselves.

Sometimes I feel overwhelmed by how many factors there are to consider in every decision I make. It can seem impossible to make a choice that is in line with all my values and that doesn't hurt anyone. At these times, I think the best I can hope to do is to make a decision that feels right in that moment and to trust in the process. This helps me cope with the crazy world we live in and to deal with the many competing factors to consider every time I make a decision.

In making the big decisions, such as where to live, and the more frequent day-to-day choices about how we live, we try to be conscious of the impact we have on this planet and other people. Every decision we make in our lives is important to the planet's sustainability and to our own personal sustainability.

I guess thinking about climate change every day of my life in my work, [but] living... so very far away, Young Friends camp is fun and nurturing, but hard to justify why that flight is so very important, so very much more important than anyone else's trips...

In seeking to live with integrity we:

        use public transport, bikes, feet, cars, taxis;

        buy local, organic, bulk, cheap as possible;

        don't consume meat, dairy, rice, wheat, alcohol;

live in group houses, near family, close to activity centres, in the country;

        …and so on and so forth.

Some of these things are mutually exclusive, which is why we don't all do all of them. Our choices are informed by the circumstances and priorities of our lives, which means that the best choice for one person is not necessarily the best choice for another. The list of things we do intentionally in our lives is endless and the specifics of it don't matter. What matters is that we are choosing to live our lives in conscious ways, with integrity and as close as we can to what we believe. We're all living our lives in different outward ways, but we are living those ways because of inward decisions we have made.

It can be hard to know how to make these choices, on what information or values to base a decision. Young Friends is a place where we see what other people are doing, see their choices and use these examples to help re-evaluate our own lives.

> *At that moment I decided that I was going to become a vegetarian. When I got home and told my parents that I was going to stop eating meat (except for eco-friendly kangaroo and sustainably fished fish!), they decided that they would join me, and the three of us have been 'kangaquarians' ever since!*

Young Friends try to let our actions arise from our values and principles. We discern where we are called to use our energies and are wary of doing service for service sake. We serve in a way that also nurtures us.

> *When we gathered at Werona [bush property near Kangaroo Valley, NSW] in January 2009, we had a pretty full agenda. We were Backhousing with a vengeance, while trying to ensure*

that there was time in our week to just be. Our time together is so precious, it brings us together and it is in the unprogrammed time that we often find the still small voice among us. Doing 'work' at Werona—for example, repairs and maintenance—is almost always on our agenda when we gather there, and this gathering was no exception. Werona is such a special place for us as a group, and for many individuals. The work we do there is an opportunity to help nurture this place that nurtures us. This is an example of how Young Friends operate and what we value.

One important thing about Quakers is that the action has a basis in being Spirit-led.

It's not just about 'Omg [Oh my God], there's this problem, let's work ourselves til we drop to fix it.' There's reflection before action. The reflection is about noticing that you're connected to something more than just you as an individual having this concern ... and that if the concern is to be acted upon, it's acted upon by more than just one person. Also, it [reflection] is a place you can come back to. Kind of like an opportunity for renewal. It might be an ideal that doesn't happen, but I think that it's there because it must happen sometimes. It's a place you can return to as rejuvenation. So it's not about unsustainable action.

We involve ourselves in organisations and groups that help nurture this planet and the people, not always in a traditional service kind of a way. It may not look like 'going out and doing good deeds for random strangers'. It takes many forms and usually involves helping our communities grow and flourish through organisations such as Frisbee teams, food co-ops, coaching, Quaker activities, and making music, and being activists for social justice through involvement with people's and rights movements.

Young Friends and 'causes'

Bob: Hey Jillian, can you believe it's only a week until Young Friends camp this year?!

Jillian: *Really?! Is that all it is?*

Bob: Yeah, hard to believe it's come so quickly.

Jillian: *Yeah. So what are you most looking forward to at camp?*

Bob: I'm looking forward to seeing Jane again, I've had a huge crush on her since last year! What about you?

Jillian: *Well, I've recently stopped buying new clothes, as you know, because of my concerns with worker conditions where the clothes are made.*

Bob: Yeah …

Jillian: *But I'm finding it really hard at the moment, there's just so much pressure from some people to dress well and wear fancy clothes. It's sometimes really hard to find quality clothes in op-shops.*

Bob: And you're wondering whether it's worth it?

Jillian: *Yeah—but I know heaps of people with similar views to mine who will be at camp, so I'm thinking maybe I can chat to them about it, see if they've had similar problems and maybe get my enthusiasm back.*

Bob: Yeah, good idea — that's such an important part of camp for me too, y'know, getting some enthusiasm back into certain parts of my life. Last year I decided to give up driving cars, and by the end of the year it was really hard, but after going to camp and chatting to people I could take a step back and look at why I was doing it in the first place — it really got my excitement back!

Jillian: *Nice one.*

Bob: Hey look, here comes Bernie.

Bernie: Hi guys, what's up?

Jillian: *We're just talking about our Quaker camp that's coming up.*

Bernie: Oh cool. Is that the one where you guys get together to save the world or something?

Bob: Well …

Jillian: *Not exactly. In fact, we don't do much of that stuff at all as a group. Heaps of people take up causes on their own, but we never seem to do it together.*

Bob: Yeah, you're right.

Bernie: Why don't you do that stuff as a group?

Bob: To be honest, I'd rather not do too much organised stuff like that at a Young Friends camp. I personally find it a better experience if we have an open agenda, and let meaningful discussions just happen when they happen, rather than forcing them to happen. We only get one or two chances a year to hang out, and it would be a shame to have too full an agenda. Often the most inspiring and important moments to do with personal causes come out of unorganised, spontaneous conversations between people.

Jillian: *Yeah, I'd agree with that. It would also be really hard to do. I mean, me and Bob are the only two Young Friends in Sydbourne. It'd be so much effort to keep in touch and coordinate stuff when we're all so spread apart.*

Bernie: Yeah, that makes sense. But surely, with so many of you having similar passions and concerns it makes sense that you'd do something as a group.

Bob: Well, it may seem like that, but our concerns and interests are also unique and personal to all of us, and it sometimes doesn't make sense to share such pursuits with a large group of people.

Bernie: But surely you can get more done as a group than on your own?

Jillian: *Not necessarily. My personal choices actually influence the people around me quite a lot. There are heaps of things we do as a group, but that's not what Young Friends is about for me. If I want to revegetate a park, I'll join a different group for that.*

Bernie: Okay, so it sounds like you guys both love the fact that camp is a place to become reinspired in your passions, so you get some enthusiasm back into that part of your life. And apart from the practical and logistical problems in taking up causes as a group, it sounds as though you don't want the few gatherings a year to be dominated by organised activities. Which makes sense — everyone likes to spend time having fun!

Work

Often our paid work is one of the ways we contribute to creating the kind of world we want to live in. Sometimes this means choosing work which pays little, working for an organisation whose values match ours, whose values we hope to influence, or that has an important role to play in an issue we are passionate about. It can be hard doing this kind of work, especially if we are working with people who don't care as much as we do, or whose values don't match our own.

For many of us, the way we do our work is also really important. It's not just about the outcome, it's also about getting there in a way that has integrity, where every voice is heard and included.

Here are some of our stories.

'The way I teach is from my Quaker principles.'

When I teach a class I am so pleased to see each person as they arrive. I greet them by name and we make a circle quickly. I expect everyone to treat the rest of the group with respect. I also expect to push each person to a new level of trust, past a point of fear or hopelessness or embarrassment.

I look at the group: Who is hanging back? Who speaks quietly? Who takes up all the space? Who is clinging to the people they feel safe with?

I find a game for that moment. Will it be something which makes them run, or laugh? Will it mean they have to cooperate with, or trust someone new? Will it require the kind of focus that brings the whole group together?

The game is always based on what the group looks like and taking them to a place where they are relaxed, comfortable about trying things with their bodies and able to work together.

Every day I teach I find someone at a point of terror ('No, I can't do that trick and I won't.'). Sometimes I know it's important for people to say 'no': girls who have just been learning to expect their 'no' to be heard in our culture and boys who are not expected to let fear stop them doing anything physical. But I try to make it safe. How can I find a simpler level of the trick so they do try it? Who in the class would they trust to 'spot' them? When I do doubles acrobatics I get both partners to try the trick with me first, then encourage them to work together.

I see the move from a face which is tight and refusing to laughing achievement.

I teach people from refugee backgrounds. Many of them walked out of their country and lived in refugee camps for years before coming here. One group I have been working with for about four years.

Adak was the shyest. She would stand about a foot out from the circle, never next to anyone. She would sit down for more than half the class. She would reel back from me if I accidentally stood too close to her. She would fold up and refuse to try doubles acrobalance (standing on someone else). This lasted three years.

Last year we did a big group show, where she worked with people from all kinds of different backgrounds. On the first day of the workshop with the new people, I divided them into groups, with people they didn't know. I turned around a moment later to find Adak standing on the shoulders of a girl she'd never met.

At the end of the show we sat in a circle and I asked people what they had learned. Adak said, 'When I met you all I didn't think that I would like you. But I've learned not to judge people by how they look.' Adak still comes to a class I teach. When we learn dance she stands at the front. When we do acrobalance she still laughs, collapses, shakes her head and says, 'Wait, wait', but she tries basing and flying—everything.

For me, everything about the way I teach is from my Quaker principles. To speak from that of God in myself to that of God in the person in front of me and to expect them to witness that of God in the rest of the group.

'My current work is nurturing to me, the plants and other people.'

The difference between my previous job in an office and the current work I do in a heritage garden couldn't be more different. The work I currently do is tangible, practical and easily visible to others. These may not always be important criteria for my work, but they are at the moment. In my previous work I was a very small, frustrated cog in a very large machine, and it was difficult to tell exactly what contribution I was making that could be worthwhile. There are only so many ways you can play around with words to make them sound the best they can. Yet with the way I prune a shrub, or when I cut back a flower or fertilise a camellia, I can see the results of this, and the extra joy is that others can see the results too. I truly feel my current work is nurturing, to me, the plants I work with, and it creates an environment other people are able to enjoy.

'I am finding ways to live out my values.'

As a child and teenager I was pushed to excel academically, and I did. I won some awards, but was left without knowing much about how to make friends, who I was, what I actually enjoyed doing or what I wanted to do with my life. As such, I followed a path of least resistance into university, then I went travelling and worked in temp jobs overseas. I had some pressure to do a PhD but I was starting to realise that I wanted to do something to help the environment. I didn't feel like I fitted in with the university department I was in, but then I had never felt I fitted in anywhere so that was nothing special.

When I was back in Australia, I received a phone call from a professor who spoke the same three languages as me (and a few more!) who wanted to know if I'd like to do some work for him in environmental health. I felt like my whole [professional] life was opening up in front of me as I realised that although I wanted to work on environmental issues, I really had to work with, about, and for people. I felt, and still do, that if I can do something to help people realise the intimate connection between their health and the health of the planet, that I might be able to help achieve some change in the way our society operates.

And so I stumbled upon the field of public health which is concerned with the wellbeing of whole populations. It is an area that suits me and I discovered a group of people with whom I feel that I fit in. At my first public heath workplace I found it was the norm to be concerned with the welfare of people, the environment and to be an advocate for women's rights, social justice and so on. I went on to undertake the first really meaningful study of my life and I am finding ways to live out my values that best utilise my skills to play my small part in creating a better world.

'Humble discernment and trust led to unexpected blessings.'

When we moved from Melbourne to Canberra I found myself facing a difficult career choice. If I was to continue pushing my technical skills, the only real options for employers were in the defence sector. Otherwise it seemed I would have to settle for a more conventional government IT job. I carried a vague feeling of unease through the process of applying and being interviewed by a maker of radars for warships. I was enthusiastic about being paid well to work with very bright people on cutting edge technology, and I reasoned that it was legitimate for Australia to hold such naval capabilities. And, after all, a radar is not a gun.

The day I pushed myself into accepting the position was followed by several sleepless nights. Eventually I gave up justifying, and faced up to the truth that this was a mistake.

Designing radar systems for warships is a legitimate activity, but it is not what I want my life's work to be contributing towards. I humbly apologised and explained my change of decision, and felt a great wave of relief and reassurance that I was now back on the right path. This path led me promptly to a job at the same pay in a more convenient location with more flexible conditions, working for the government on a project with an environmental bent, with a great boss who can give me better opportunities to develop new skills in areas I hadn't previously imagined finding interesting. A little bit of humble discernment and trust opened the way for some unexpected blessings.

Relationships

Young Friends provides us with a real chance to get to know one other in new and unexpected ways that push beyond the normal limits of friendship. This informs the ways we think about ourselves and interact with people in other parts of our lives. The opportunity to develop deep friendships through Young Friends can strengthen relationships in other parts of our lives.

> *I have an idea in my head that people aren't open-minded and accepting of new things. Whether or not this is true is somewhat irrelevant—people can't be open-minded and accepting until they're given the chance to be!*

Young Friends is a place where many of us have experienced and practised this open-mindedness. Expecting to find goodness in all people transforms our lives and the way we interact with our friends, family and colleagues.

> *Continually I question whether this friend is worth the effort, yet I know I am unable to write him off as a lost cause. I know there is that of God in him, as in us all. Also, too, I am aware that many people I have known may have thought similar of me, yet they did not give up. And so, I know that I must persist, because there is always hope.*

Answering that of God in everyone can be a real challenge, especially when you realise that it applies to people you may not like or respect.

> *I think before that I had always assumed that there was 'that of God in everyone that I like' or 'that of God in everyone who is nice'. Realising 'that of God in everyone' truly did apply to everyone changed my view of the world quite a lot. I like to think of 'that of God in everyone' also meaning that there is that of good in everyone. Everyone has the capacity to be good, and everyone also has the capacity to change.*

Appreciating this capacity for goodness in others also leads to recognition of the (sometimes) challenging concept that this also applies to ourselves. As one Young Friend said:

> *I suddenly realised that if there is that of God in everyone, then there must be that of God in me!*

Challenges to living out in the world

A n important part of being a Young Friend is the attempt to live with integrity, in a way that gives voice to the Quaker principles we value. Yet, as with anything, there are challenges. Some challenges come from the world we live in (its influences, expectations and pace of life), some are specific to being young people, and others are struggles we create all by ourselves.

Children of our times

Living in the modern world deeply affects who we are. And, for young people, life in this world can seem a bit in-between. In many cases we have left our family homes, and until we 'settle' and create our own home, we feel a bit homeless. Where, in this time of studies, travel, meeting partners and beginning careers is 'home'?

As we grow into our place in the world, there is potential for the communities we know to become less relevant. Our childhood influences and interests give way to 'real life' and new experiences as we find our own way and this can affect our sense of belonging among Quakers. Many of us experience a time of questioning and seeking as we finish school and begin university or careers. We begin to question the beliefs and principles we were brought up with and look for something that speaks clearly to each of us as individuals.

The one community we all have in common, Young Friends, encourages individual thought and discovery. We value this, but find it leads some of us to a place of isolation, a lack of a true sense of community and a spiritual loneliness. This includes both Young Friends who have grown up in the Society, and those who have come to Quakers as young adult seekers. For the latter, the initial excitement of discovering Quakers can give way to a sense of bewilderment when long periods of attendance don't always lead to a deeper understanding of the Quaker way.

Saying you're a Quaker can lead to being put into a religious box, even among open-minded friends. All Quakers face this, but perhaps Young Friends face it more deeply, given the questioning among our peers about whether organised religion and spirituality is relevant anymore, even where it is as loosely organised as Quakers. We face a temptation to downplay the Quaker motivations for our actions, and justify the way we live in other terms. This outward downplaying may lead to a diminishing connection to the Quaker principles that we seek to live inwardly. Are people right to question organised religion? Do we really need the Society to live a 'good' life anymore?

> 'Do you tell people that you are a Quaker?' I tell people I know reasonably well but usually not people I've only just met. The reason is that most people I meet have never heard of Quakers and get them a bit confused with the Amish or other very conservative religions. They then seem to feel that I will be judging them or they assume that they can guess my attitude/ideas/philosophy on life. I prefer not to be put in a box (particularly when it's the wrong box!) by someone I've just met. I prefer they get to know me for who I am instead of guessing who they think I am.

In addition to these challenges, Young Friends in Australia also realise that many of us are born into positions of great privilege compared to people in the rest of the world. Most of us are white, well educated, with English as our first language. We are questioning whether this means our actions, although appearing edgy and liberal to our peers, do in fact actually help the most marginalised in our society, and in the world. Without realising it, we are complicit in, and benefactors of, established power structures because of our language, education and wealth, and we won't ever really be able to experience life as most people in the world do. Yet, like our spiritual forebears, we humbly choose to try to act and change the world, using our access and privilege to work with all humanity. This goes hand in hand with our efforts to grow and change ourselves.

Searching for stillness

This world is a loud place, with 24-hour media, multi-billion dollar advertising industries, and opinions all over daily newspapers, blogs and billboards. Everyone is competing to be heard and so few have time to listen. We can't escape it and still live in the world.

The language we grow up with, and hear all around us is that of power, dominion, war, anger. Language influences the way all of us think. Quakers have realised this since our earliest days. Young Friends are inspired by this — inspired that Quakers see the possibility of a different reality and seek to live it here and now. Yet we question: how can we reclaim a peaceful, egalitarian language and get our words out there so that they grow to shape the world? What is our 21st Century 'plain speak'?

Perhaps our loudest 'proclamation' is silence! Perhaps the most prophetic thing we can do is to choose not to add to the wordiness of the world. If there is one thing some of us have found that sets us apart as Quakers, it is not finding silence weird. General Australian culture finds silence around others almost intolerable and there is a strong need to fill every gap. Yet we feel Quakers continue to offer an alternative.

Being a Quaker means having a space in my life where I take time to slow down and try to find stillness.

Slowing down also seems a constant challenge. We are so busy! There isn't always time for the silence or the vital relationships that keep us going. This is why camp is such a meaningful time for many Young Friends. It is a week of uninterrupted community, where there is enough time to relax and really connect with others, although even here we struggle with having too much to do and not enough time to do it in.

> *I find I have to actively put the stillness first and the busyness last in order to have any stillness. Sometimes it is hard to remember that the world doesn't come first. I don't think I'm any more along there than any Young Friend, or any Quaker. I think maybe Young Friends have the advantage that there are people less busy among them. I remember being grabbed by another Young Friend at Yearly Meeting and taken off to sit around and spend half a morning learning Tibetan throat singing (a kind of guttural droning hum). The sense of freedom and serious unseriousness was great; who cared what meeting sessions I was missing? So maybe what we all need is a personal silence trainer or someone to remind us not to take our busyness seriously.*

Unfortunately, for young active and involved people, sometimes the current way that the Society is organised doesn't allow us enough space to really cultivate silence. With our busy lives in an even busier world, time is precious. If membership of the Society is measured by joining more committees or attending more meetings, we don't want to do this, or have the time to. We would value more opportunity for stillness within the Society, as well as outside it.

Our Quaker identity

How has being a Friend changed the way we live?

Edgar: The first thing that appealed to me about Friends and made me attend Meeting was not that I wanted to change, but that I'd found a community that was, in fact, very similar to me. However, having been an attender now for three years, and enjoyed the safe feeling of being 'at home' with the Meeting and especially the Young Friends, I am beginning to wish that the community would challenge me to live out the Truth in my life in new and different ways.

Fernando: *As a Young Friend who grew up in the Society, when I initially thought about this question, I was unsure how to answer it. Being a Friend is all that I know—it's who I am and how I was taught to live. Gradually, though, as I've grown up I have begun to see that, in fact, it has changed the way I live. A recent trip to a world Quaker gathering showed me 'strangers' from contexts vastly different to my own, yet with so many similarities in the way we tried to live out in the world.*

A work colleague unfamiliar with my Quaker background once asked me why it was that I tried to work for justice in everything I did. When I explained it to her, I realised that I live that way because of our testimonies. So my life has changed because of Friends. At first I didn't realise it, and it may have seemed 'the norm', but, as I've grown and met other Friends and non-Friends, I can definitely see the impact it's had on my life.

Gretel: Being a Friend definitely changed the way I live. Probably the most concrete change was changing my course at university from something that would make a lot of money to training for a career that would let me make a difference in people's lives. Young Friends camps have been a great place to be honest about who I am and explore what I believe and stand for. And, lastly, I think Friends is slowly making me a vegetarian!

Hansel: *Well, I was initially drawn to Quakers because of the history and legacy of the early Quakers, and the way they lived out their faith. Unfortunately, though, what I found was far from the ideal community I'd read about or created in my head. I had some difficult experiences with the group and had my feelings hurt due to an incident on camp. In my mind, the Young Friends spoke all the right words about equality and honesty and integrity, but failed to live up to them. I have left Friends because I did not want to become like that, and am undertaking this journey of life on my own again.*

Inga: I grew up in the Society but I never really got involved in Young Friends. I really value the Quaker ideals of seeing the Light in everyone and speaking for change. These have definitely shaped who I am and are still a daily part of my life even though I'm not involved with Quakers anymore.

Being Quakers

Young Friends minus Quakerism would not be the same group that it is: the thing that holds it together is Quakerism.

Much of our Quaker identity is based in and inspired by the same things that inspire other members of the Society of Friends such as Quaker history, testimonies and worship practices. A fundamental belief that is core to Young Friends is that there is that of God, or goodness, in all people. This is central to feeling a connection to Quakers and forms the basis for our interactions with each other and the wider community.

We value Quaker testimonies and they inform the way we relate to other people and to ourselves.

The equality testimony means a lot to me. I grew up in Quakers and I have known since I was very small that I, as a woman, can do whatever the heck I want!... I can remember the time when I met someone who didn't have that confidence, and I thought, 'Oh' ... Quakers were one of the first religions to have women involved in the same capacities as men. Women were allowed to minister. For me, that has really influenced and improved my life because it's a confidence that I don't even question.

We are inspired by Quaker history and by stories about early Friends. At that time the Quaker way was a new and radical discovery—a dangerous yet liberating discovery. Quakers spoke with a clarity and urgency that could only come from direct experience.

Put yourself under the Light and examine all the dark corners and scrutinise yourself. Shine the Light in all the dark corners and find where you're going wrong and where you need to improve. It's a harsh process but it's one that we don't get exposed to in other parts of our lives. It's a healthy balance to the 'comfortableness' and sitting on your laurels. I like the interrogative aspect of Quakerism.

Like other Friends, we also struggle with the need to rediscover what these early stories mean for us now.

We are inspired by the way that Quakers live out their values in practical social activism, and by the sense that this is something anyone can do. We are empowered knowing that we do not need to be any more than we already are, or can be, to do this. It gives us courage to know that we can all experience leadings and live them out in our own lives.

The Quaker faith gives us a basis or structure within which to explore our own spirituality. It gives us the concepts and language to make sense of the world and its conflicts, to approach spiritual questions and to understand other faiths. Young Friends and our local Meetings provide a safe place and open-minded people to explore spiritual matters with.

I find it hard to live consciously and from the heart all the time. I am not the full person I want to be. Being part of Friends gives me the space to find more of who I want to be. It gives me access to amazing people, amazing processes, amazing books, amazing experiences.

It is important to Young Friends that Quakers are open to engaging with, and finding the good in other faith groups. That we could belong to Quakers as well as another religious group makes sense and tells us that we, as well as others, are welcome in the community. In the same way, the support within the Quaker community for queer people and relationships is crucial to our feeling comfortable in associating with, and identifying as, Young Friends.

The meaning of Meeting for Worship

We value the practice of Quaker Meeting for Worship. It is a chance to experience stillness and renewal in the midst of a busy life. Worship is also an essential balance to social activism.

More than one person doing it. More than act, act, act, burn out. Reflection, action, reflection, action. It's a continuous process. Like a battery recharging.
That's what a Quaker meeting can be about. Not always, and not for all people, but it can play that role. It's on every week (regardless of whether you go, it helps us all to know it's there).

The Quaker Meeting is a simple form of worship that can be accessible to everyone, everywhere. At Young Friends camp we work as a group to make it accessible to all by choosing a time when most people will be awake and free, and selecting a location and seating types that will meet the needs of those who are there. Even then, not all Young Friends choose to attend, but also feel free to hold Meetings for Worship at camp in addition to the one that is organised for the whole group.

Many Young Friends have had experience with groups such as Zen Buddhists and other Christian churches and are familiar with various meditation practices. Quaker Meetings can be a bit difficult initially for some, but for others are not particularly strange because we have been somewhere similar, or because we have been looking for something like Meeting for Worship.

> *Discovering such a simple method of worship was a true blessing to me—I didn't have to worry about knowing when to stand up and sit down, or the words to say. I learnt to listen in silence to the Light within.*

Despite this, it is a fact that few Young Friends attend their local Meeting regularly. The reasons for this are diverse. Some Young Friends have other commitments or live far away from their local Meeting House. Others feel that while being a Quaker is important to them, a weekly Meeting for Worship is not a priority in their life at the moment. Some Young Friends feel that their local Meeting is currently not meeting their needs, while others often struggle in Meeting, but continue to attend.

It is interesting to note that Young Friends often struggle with the same things that other Friends also find difficult in Meeting. Advices and Queries reminds us that we are not alone in sometimes struggling to become centred, to accept vocal ministry that doesn't speak to us and to find a balance between worship and business, or busyness, in the life of the Meeting.

We have spent a lot of time listening to different perspectives within the Young Friends group, and invite you to listen with us ...

Jemima & Kenji

Jemima: I don't attend my local Meeting very often—but I love it when I do. I feel a sense of home when I'm there. But with work, family and friends and all the other things in my life, often a free Sunday morning is actually all I want.

Kenji: *Do you miss feeling part of the community?*

Jemima: I suppose I get that sense of regular community support more from Young Friends at the moment. I'm lucky to live close to a few Young Friends and we hang out quite a lot. Also, I always go to Meeting for Worship when I'm travelling interstate—I love catching up with all the great people I know from Yearly Meeting.

Kenji: *Yearly Meeting is really important to me too. I love all the people I meet there, you take time out from normal life, and everyone's really inspired about being Quakers. I love feeling a part of such a passionate group. Going to Summer School, and the chance to have those surreal, life-changing conversations at 2 am while eating chocolate on the roof!*

Jemima: Do you go to your local Meeting?

Kenji: *Not often, I only go a few times a year. I don't really enjoy it when I do go. I keep trying, but it doesn't really get any better. I guess I'm just not at that stage of life right now. I guess I feel like being a Quaker is more about how I live my life every day.*

Lobelia & Mustafa

Lobelia: I go to Meeting for Worship pretty much every week—and often I'm the only person in the room who's under 40. For me, it's an important space for reflection in the midst of a busy life. It feels really natural to me, it's like: if you are looking for an experience of the Divine, how else could you ever approach it other than through silence?

Mustafa: *I love the silence too—but I rarely go to Meeting. I'd like my local Meeting to be my main Quaker community, but I really struggle with it at the moment. Partly because it's a large group, and partly because I see some really obvious patterns in the Meeting — like when the same Friend ministers every week. It's like we forget the true reason why we're there. Sometimes Young Friends hold an evening Meeting for Worship in each others' homes — I often go to that and it has become really important for me.*

Lobelia: How is it different from your local Meeting?

Mustafa: *Being a much smaller group is important — and having really genuine, strong relationships with everyone there. At my local Meeting it's always more of an individual experience because I don't know the people and their concerns very well. With Young Friends I get more of a sense of the group, I know the people and can pray for specific things that I know they are struggling with.*

Lobelia: That's how it was for early Quakers — holding Meeting in people's homes. It's interesting that you prefer the smaller group. Whenever I've been in a smaller Meeting I find I miss the energy of the bigger group.

Mustafa: *It's also because in a small group the moment when worship ends is much more gentle. Sometimes at my local Meeting it's like we shake hands and then you're expected to move straight from deep worship and letting go of self into smiling and wishing everyone good morning! It's quite a shock. Everyone starts talking all at once, then all the unimportant notices have to be read out right now, then we all have to rush to the tearoom and talk at nineteen to the dozen to catch up on all the important news of life and community.*

Lobelia: Yeah, that feeling of 'busyness' is a big problem. There are times when my local Meeting feels more like an activist organisation than a spiritual community. When I think of the older Quakers at my local Meeting, their energy and faith in the world is one of the things that's so inspiring. It's ironic that this also means they are sometimes too busy to get to know new people — or they take on too much and get burnt out.

Mustafa: *I guess Young Friends struggle with that too. Sometimes we do okay. During the process of writing this lecture we've done pretty well, I think. We've worked so hard, but it's been really important to put aside time for worship and reflection — and for socialising as well. It nurtures the relationships between us — which are kind of what the lecture's all about anyway.*

Nathan & Olga

Nathan: My local Meeting is really important to me. Because I didn't grow up with Friends I wouldn't feel like a Quaker if I didn't go to Meeting.

Olga: *Does it bother you that everyone's about 20 years older than you?*

Nathan: It's hard, especially when you get comments like 'It's just so wonderful to see a young person here'. I know it's well intentioned, but it kind of doesn't leave room for me to be myself, and to participate as an individual, rather than just a 'young person'. And it just takes longer to get to know people who are your parents' age — you just have less in common.

Olga: *Yeah, I know what you mean.*

Nathan: You grew up in Quakers, right? I've always thought it must have been great to grow up in Quakers.

Olga: *Yeah, it's kind of the opposite for me: I don't go to Meeting much because people know me too well. I feel like they all see me as the same kid I was 10 years ago.*

Learning what it means to be a Quaker

> *I didn't like being the main one responsible for explaining Quaker stuff, because I don't think I'm an expert, and anyway if you ask 100 Quakers what Quakers are about you'll get 101 answers.*

As with Meeting for Worship, many Young Friends have very different experiences of learning about Quakers and what it means to be part of the Religious Society of Friends. As one of the discerning marks of being a Quaker is an emphasis on living with integrity rather than focusing on what we believe, we sometimes feel left to fumble our way through the silence of Meeting as we try to find out 'what to do'. The relative lack of any structured teaching, mentorship, or explanation can make being a member of the group simultaneously challenging and freeing. It can also be a really freeing opportunity to have this area of our life where no-one is telling us what to do and we get to figure things out at our own pace, in our own way.

Most Young Friends who grew up in the Society learned about being a Quaker through the way their parents brought them up and through attending Children's Meeting.

> *The main way I have learned about being a Quaker has been by being intimate with my mother's spiritual journey. She has been sharing with me her struggles, her joys and her learnings since before she went back to Friends when I was 11. Sometimes I wish she wouldn't. Usually I am interested in her, the person, rather than what is a Quaker and how can I be one? But every discovery of hers, every battle with herself, new way of being in the world teaches me something. To be so close to someone else's spiritual journey is such a rich way to learn. I feel like this kind of understanding is enough for me and I am satisfied without another form of structured learning.*

While some are happy without formal instruction, for others, a lack of formal teaching of Quaker process and spiritual practices is a hindrance to meaningful engagement with local Meetings and the broader Society and leads us to wonder if this is why some young people end up looking elsewhere for spiritual community.

> *How can they [Young Friends who are brought up in the Society] want to stay on if they are left only with the teaching they had as little kids? Perhaps more than that, maybe they need honest teaching and more reflection from*

the older people. They need to know what Quakers actually
believe and to see people striving. I wonder sometimes if
Young Friends don't stay in the Society because they learn
an ideal form of Quakerism when they are children but find
the Society something quite different altogether. Maybe the
problem is that they are taught where the adults aren't!!!
Maybe they just need space to move away and come back
again — but they need a reason to come back.

This is reflected in the way that some of us who grew up in the Society answer the question 'What is a Quaker?', which is to talk about history, about our radical roots and what early Quakers did/said/believed. We realise that actually sometimes this has little or no significance to us at the moment, and that we need to rediscover why we do these things now. Others who joined the Society as young adults are more likely to describe Quakers in terms of practices such as Meeting for Worship and what we gain from being a part of the Society.

I feel really resourced by my Meeting and by Young Friends.
I don't think that I know all I want to know or have learnt
all I need to learn about Quakerism, but I do think that the
information is available, and willingly offered by Quakers,
albeit in mostly informal ways. I find the informal learning
the best; that's when someone just tells a story or we have a
conversation about how to live as a Quaker.

Growing up, growing out of Young Friends

What happens when one 'graduates' from Young Friends? A large proportion of the current group of Young Friends is around, or approaching, 30 years old — the age at which people tend to start thinking about leaving the group. These Young Friends are going through a period of questioning about 'What next?'. Many realise that their relationship with Quakers will change, and are exploring the varying paths.

For some Young Friends, this 'graduation' will entail following many before them along a path that does not involve regular contact with the Society. As has already been mentioned, the heart of Quaker experience for many Young Friends is the yearly camp, rather than weekly Meeting for Worship. This is probably a large reason why many Young Friends do not transition into the broader Society when they get too old to participate in Young Friends. The relationships in a tight-knit, small group built from relaxed unstructured time spent together at camp will be very different from the community built from weekly Meetings for Worship and committees.

> *If the core place of belonging for Young Friends is camp, and the majority of Young Friends have never really been connected to Meeting, then why are we surprised that when they are 'finished' with Young Friends they leave and don't return? Why should they now join a group that they didn't feel a part of when they were in the community? No wonder they leave.*

Although it is sad to see people leave the Society, it does bother us that we feel somehow called to account for the fact that Young Friends often leave.

> *It concerns me that Young Friends now have to account for this state. And the Young Friends that are doing the account, or the lecture, are the ones who remained, who found something, and as such can't really speak on behalf of those who didn't.*

> *... Can we not trust that the Truth will continue to prosper, even after all the Young Friends have stopped being Young Friends? Yes, we can teach and tell people, and share our values, not to save the Society, but to share them because they are truthful and life-giving. How our sharing is received, or lived out, is not up to us. It may well mean people join*

> *the Society, or they live the Truth out in other ways, with no connection to our institution.*

Other Young Friends are confident about being more involved with their local Meetings.

> *... after this lecture is done I'd like to stop being a Young Friend and be more confident and do other 'mainstream' Quaker activities. Maybe I'll join a committee.*

A challenge for Young Friends leaving the group and having only their local Meeting as their Quaker community is that, despite being in their thirties, there is usually a substantial age gap between them and the next youngest members or attenders. While many Young Friends appreciate the contact they have had through Quakers with people of all ages, and feel confident and comfortable in an environment with people of different ages, attending Meeting is a different experience when we have others of a similar age and/or life stage around.

Young Friends would like to see the sense of community we have, the support we give to one another, and the strength we draw from that, continue throughout and beyond the time we identify as Young Friends. We recognise that maintaining the sense of community when each of us moves beyond the vague '30-ish' upper age limit of Young Friends will be challenging. We will not find direct replicas of our experiences at camps and dhal nights in the broader body of the Society, but wish to explore new ways of being together in this next stage of life.

Finally, we recognise that it is important that we do move on, as many have before us, to make space for new Young Friends to create their experience.

Vision for the future

What we've written in this lecture might be seen by many to be a glimpse into the future of the Society. Perhaps the trends among Young Friends, in what concerns us and how we practise as Quakers, will grow to enrich, infuse and guide the Society in decades to come. We have tried, throughout our Backhouse preparation, to discern a sense of where Young Friends see the Society going and where we would like it to go, and to reflect our diversity with a unified voice.

Early in the process, we wondered whether there might be a grand vision for the future, as yet unarticulated among Young Friends. Some of us thought this might emerge as the lecture developed. What we found was something more real and, perhaps, more complex than a single grand vision for the future — we have found a common hope.

Young Friends are hopeful about the future—about our future as individuals and as Quakers, and in the wider world. This has come up again and again as we worked to find a unified voice. For example, when we gathered at Camp Cottermouth outside Canberra over the 2009 Easter long weekend we were guided through some theatre sport exercises. In groups of three and four we responded to various questions about the future by making still-life sculptures with our bodies. Many of us were struck with how positive most of the responses were. While there were some questioning and uncertain responses, some Young Friends even managed to respond with hope to the question of how we saw the future of global politics. The future remains, from the perspective of Young Friends, pretty bright and colourful. As one Young Friend said,

> *I'm just happy that no one thinks we're going to be dead and dying and dismembered and in nuclear war and frying in the heat.*

Our common hope grows out of our experiences of the Young Friends community. We hope we can keep this sense of sacred friendship, growth, challenge and fun going as we walk our diverse (and possibly divergent) paths into the future.

Those of us reaching the age of moving on wonder, 'Can our experiences in Young Friends translate to the broader Quaker community?'. We can give no answer yet. Some Young Friends felt the Backhouse Lecture would be an opportunity to challenge some of the long-held customs of the Society that had become stale and could be re-examined. We also felt this expectation from other Quakers.

> *But before we have a message we need an identity. We can only find our message in ourselves (Who can pass on a message they don't believe in?). So what do we actually believe, as a group? Can we agree on it? I think a genuine spiritual worship, freedom from dogma, finding of personal truths, putting our principles into practice are things anyone can appreciate.*

We heard a number of Young Friends express a hope to see the Society open up and become less isolated — to rediscover the universality of our message. And as technology continues to develop, the Society has potential to become more international, with more enriching connections to Friends and Young Friends overseas.

The simplest hope, and perhaps the most deeply felt, was that we can find more ways to get to know each and every one of us, Young Friends and older, on a deeper level. The experience of Young Friends offers possibilities for the broader Society and we look forward to continuing to share these with Quakers.

It is worth remembering, though, that the hopes of Young Friends in 2010 do not represent the totality of the future of the Society. Many Young Friends today will not be Friends in years to come. We are but a partial glimpse of the future. Many of us will drift from the Society once we pass from Young Friends, as Young Friends often have in the past. And many new Friends of all ages will join in years to come, bringing with them new perspectives, hopes and needs.

In the end, we are all Friends, younger and older. Young Friends can say we are prepared to trust in where the sense of the community is leading. Perhaps the Society will grow exponentially, or perhaps it will reach a stage, corporately or in our own lives, where it is time to lay it down and seek something new. There are more important and immediate things to do than worry too much about such questions now.

The Quaker way offers us all the remarkable chance to create the world we want to see, right here, right now, and have the full support of a loving community. Writing the Backhouse Lecture has shown this to us very clearly, and in some cases opened our eyes to something we may have taken for granted. We hope it has for all who read it too. In such company, we are prepared to trust with our community, seek to live true to ourselves in every moment, forgive ourselves for sometimes failing in this, and work to create the Society of the future with joyful expectation and excitement about the possibilities ahead.

Appendix 1: Canberra Young Friends' story

When I came to Canberra, I wanted to have a regular gathering of young people with whom I could be open and relaxed at my house. I had experienced something similar in Melbourne called 'dhal night', which was the result of an initiative started through the Student Christian Movement but which had become a non-religious friendship group that attracted many of the Young Friends in Melbourne. It was the main way I had got to know Young Friends in Melbourne. Also, I had been feeling led to hold some kind of spiritual gathering at my home for some time but the way had not yet become clear on how I should do that. I decided to just start with inviting young Canberra Quakers to my first 'dhal night' in Canberra and see what happened.

Shortly after we started the regular fortnightly gatherings, Young Friends were invited to consider being the Backhouse Lecturers in 2010. We used the dhal nights to talk about this, including the idea that we, as a group, might take on a facilitation role. We could see that having a regular gathering would enable us to undertake a more substantial role than individual Young Friends would be able to do in other parts of the country and that without some kind of lead group, it would be too hard for Australian Young Friends to do the lecture.

The decision to offer to facilitate the lecture process was not taken lightly by Canberra Young Friends. It was an act of faithfulness by a small, new group, who hardly knew each other. We knew that taking on the task was an outrageous, but right, thing to do.

During the year that followed, the Canberra Young Friends group grew probably more than any other Quaker group in the country. We welcomed many new people into our midst, most of whom have stayed while some have moved away. Our diversity in age, gender, Quaker experience and degrees of connection to both other Young Friends in Australia and the local Canberra Meeting has been hugely important. Having some people well versed in Quaker history, theology and practice as well as people very new to Quakerism has facilitated learning and lots of fun.

A key factor in our success is that a number of us regularly attend the local Meeting for Worship, and meet new young people to invite to our gatherings. We take particular care to keep inviting those who haven't been very involved and offering lifts to people without easy transport options.

We meet once a fortnight, which is sufficient to maintain contact but not so frequent as to become a burden. Vegetarian, gluten- and dairy-free food is always provided for free. The size of the group is crucial. We are small enough that we can tune into where each person is at, and there is time and space to hear from the quiet people in the group. We can form meaningful relationships and the group is also big enough that even if quite a few people do not feel like coming along one night, it doesn't leave the group too diminished.

Having time together doing 'not work' has been really important and is one of the key things about Young Friends that makes us work as a community. We also hold Meeting for Worship before dinner — a special time for those who can or want to come along.

Appendix 2: Dhal recipes

Ben's standard dhal

We cook up a three-times batch to feed ten people, or to feed the two of us for several days. We serve it with a dollop of plain yoghurt, chopped fresh coriander, and maybe some spicy mango chutney or similar if we're feeling extravagant. None of the measurements matter much, just chuck it in—it will work.

Where to find it: Solomon C 1990, *Charmaine Solomon's Complete Vegetarian Cookbook.* HarperCollins, Sydney. See Lentil puree, p. 339.

Ben's more popular chickpea dhal

Where to find it: Stephen W, Blayney D, Price J (eds) 2004, *The Essential Vegetarian Cookbook,* Murdoch Books, Millers Point. See Chickpea curry, p. 134.

Evan's Ethiopian dhal

Also known as Misr Wat (Ethiopian spiced red lentils)
Serves 4.
Where to find it:
http://www.thetartan.org/2004/10/11/pillbox/cuisineabayethiopiansliberty
(Accessed 30 Aug 2009)

Gareth's first dhal

Prep time 15 mins, cooking time 1 hour 15 mins, serves 8.
Where to find it: Clark, Pamela 2006, *The Australian Women's Weekly Cook: How to Cook Absolutely Everything,* ACP Magazines, Sydney. See p. 396.

Sal's basic dhal

A housemate taught me this when I lived in international student accommodation.

Cook about half an onion and some garlic in ghee or plain vege oil.

Add a chopped tomato or a part/whole tin of chopped tomatoes. Simmer and reduce as long as you can be bothered (or not at all) adding extra water as you go.

Pour in a cup of room temperature water, then add your spices. I usually use about 1 tsp turmeric, <1 tsp coriander powder, 1.5 tsp cumin powder, pinch hot chilli powder, 1/2 tsp garam masala, 1/2 tsp salt, grind of pepper.

Finally, add cooked lentils of your choice (don't forget to drain and discard the soaking and cooking water), and/or vegetables such as cauliflower, potato, mushroom, zucchini, carrot, peas. If adding vegetables, just add in order of how long they will take to cook.

I like to eat this with fresh coriander and natural (full cream!) yoghurt.

Em's dahl

Heat oil and Nuttelex, add about a teaspoon of mustard seeds; when they start to pop, add about a tablespoon of cumin, as much chilli as you can stand, dried coriander, turmeric, and anything else that smells right.

Mix it all up, then add onions. When onions are nearly cooked, add garlic and ginger.

I like to put a vegetable in my dahl, so usually add pumpkin at this point (and sometimes coconut milk or tin of tomatoes).

Cook for a few minutes, then add red lentils and salt.

Mix, then add water.

Cook until lentils are done, add lemon juice (at least half a lemon) and spinach if you've got some.

Great with lime pickle.

Appendix 3: Name round ideas

At nearly all of our gatherings, Young Friends begin proceedings with a name round to introduce ourselves. Below are some of the favourite things we ask everyone to tell the group along with their name. Even when we all know each other, we often start by going around the circle and saying something about how we are or what our day or week has been like. This way everyone has an opportunity to speak and we can tune into how others are feeling.

- Favourite scar
- Something good from today
- Something I'm grateful for
- Favourite vegetable
- If I had a superpower it would be…
- Score of how you're doing out of 100
- Name, claim, drop (make up a 'name' for yourself that describes how you're going, 'claim' something good from your day, 'drop' something that will prevent you from being present with the group)
- Favourite dip
- The story of your name
- Something nobody here knows about me is…
- Two truths and a lie (everyone says three things about themselves, two of which are true and one that is made up. Everyone then guesses which one is not true)
- What I had for breakfast today
- Something I like about the person next to me is…
- Three words about how I'm going
- Favourite type of cake
- My favourite name game is…

Appendix 4:
Our cover tells a story

I took the photograph on the cover at Cape Conran, just east of Lakes Entrance in Victoria in 2005. I had been slowly exploring down the east coast all the way from Brisbane, taking weeks and weeks over it. So, on the day I reached the south-east corner of Victoria, I went for a walk round the east cape of Cape Conran. I scrambled around the headland to the outermost point—miles and miles from anywhere it seemed. And there were the rocks. It was entrancing, magical, peaceful, alive, fragile yet strong and steady, a fleeting thing in the scale of geology and yet timeless at the same time.

Someone once told me that in some parts of the world a stack of stones is a symbol of peace and meditation, or a shrine even. I heard a story of a mountain somewhere where pilgrims bring a stone from their home place to leave in stacks like this, as a message that they have been there, as an act of community with other pilgrims that they may never have met. Each adding to another stack or starting a new one, building unity through time. Leaving something of their home there, instead of taking something away. Each one telling a story, yet one that can only be fully read by the giver.

Janice Sheen

www.ingramcontent.com/pod-product-compliance
Lightning Source LLC
La Vergne TN
LVHW041207080426
835508LV00008B/847